Zanaida Stewart Robles

MAGNIFICAT
AND NUNC DIMITTIS

SATB | PIANO AND ORGAN

VOCAL SCORE

OXFORD
UNIVERSITY PRESS

OXFORD
UNIVERSITY PRESS

Great Clarendon Street, Oxford OX2 6DP,
United Kingdom

Oxford University Press is a department of the University of Oxford.
It furthers the University's objective of excellence in research, scholarship,
and education by publishing worldwide. Oxford is a registered trade mark of
Oxford University Press in the UK and in certain other countries

First published 2023

Impression: 1

ISBN 978–0–19–356329–2

Music and text origination by Andrew Jones
Printed in Great Britain on acid-free paper by
Halstan & Co. Ltd, Amersham, Bucks.

Composer's note

My Magnificat and Nunc Dimittis were originally scored for SATB choir with both piano and organ accompaniment, as presented here. The piano and organ combination is a nod to the Black American church in which I grew up, where both instruments were used simultaneously for almost all music during church services (typically gospel music). All Saints Episcopal Church in Pasadena, California, for which my Magnificat and Nunc Dimittis were composed, also had a tradition of using both piano and organ with various styles for special occasions. Because of my study and work in the Episcopal church, my Magnificat and Nunc Dimittis are firmly rooted in the Western classical music tradition, heavily influenced by the works of Howells, Vaughan Williams, and Holst. The harmony, form, and melodic elements in both pieces employ heavy usage of the octatonic scale: an 8-note scale constructed by alternating semitones/half steps and tones/whole steps.

This note may be reproduced as required for programme notes.

Duration: Magnificat 5.5 minutes; Nunc Dimittis 6 minutes

This piece is also available in a version for SATB and organ only (ISBN 978–0–19–356507–4).

Magnificat

Luke 1: 46–55

ZANAIDA STEWART ROBLES

Duration: 5.5 mins

Glo - ry be____ to the Fa - ther, and to the Son, and to the Ho - ly Spi - rit;____

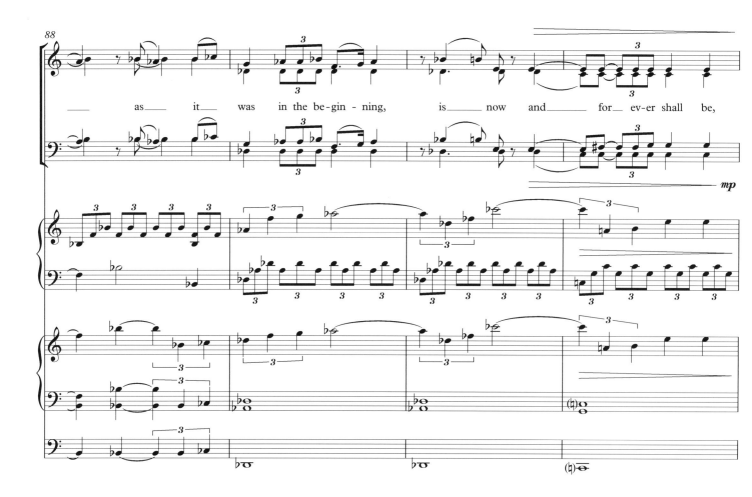

____ as____ it was in the be-gin - ning, is____ now and____ for__ ev-er shall be,

world_____ with - out end, world with - out end, world with - out end,

world_____ with - out end, world with - out end, world with - out end.

Nunc Dimittis

Luke 2: 29–32

Duration: 6 mins

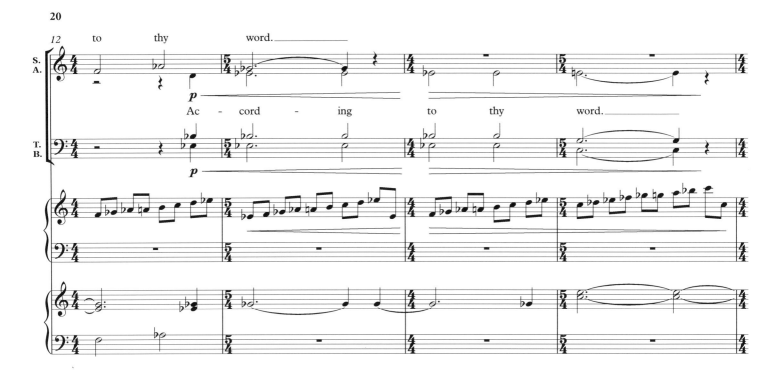

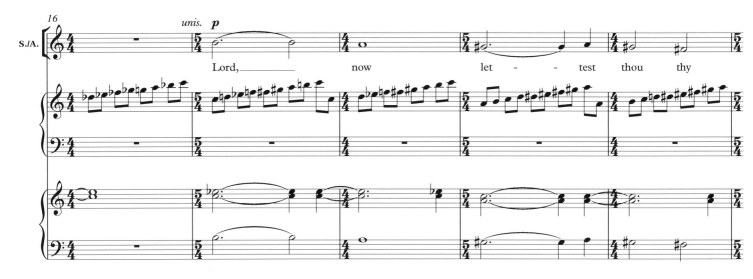

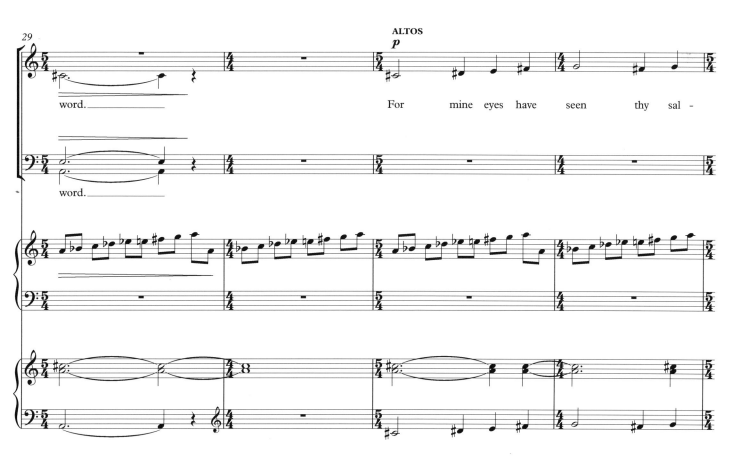

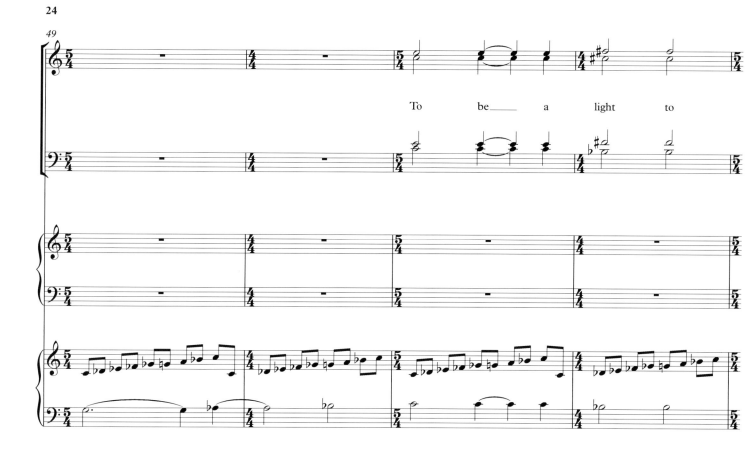

To be___ a light to

light - en___ the Gen - tiles, And to be_____ the

Ped.

Man.

glo - ry, to be _____ the glo - ry, the

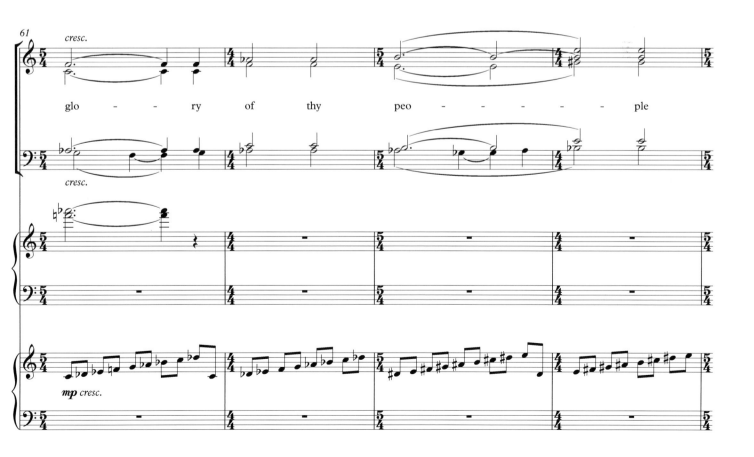

glo - - ry of thy peo - - - - - ple

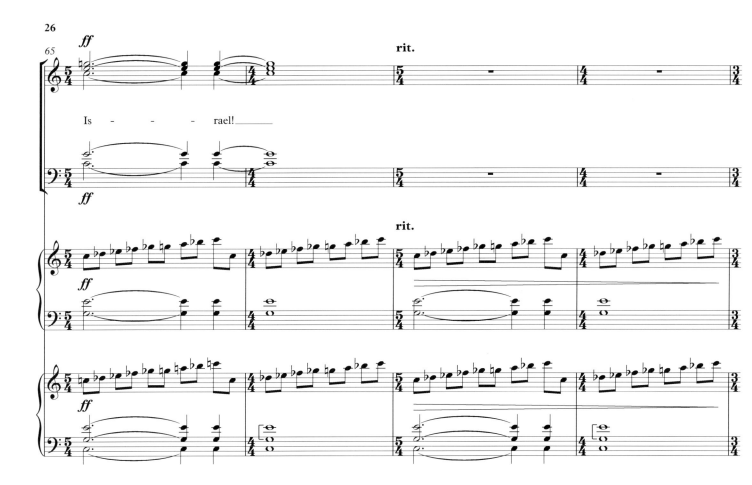

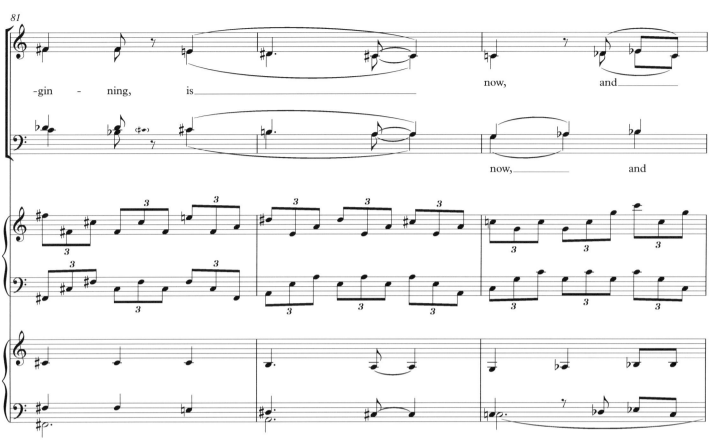

-gin - ning, is _____ now, _____ and _____

now, _____ and

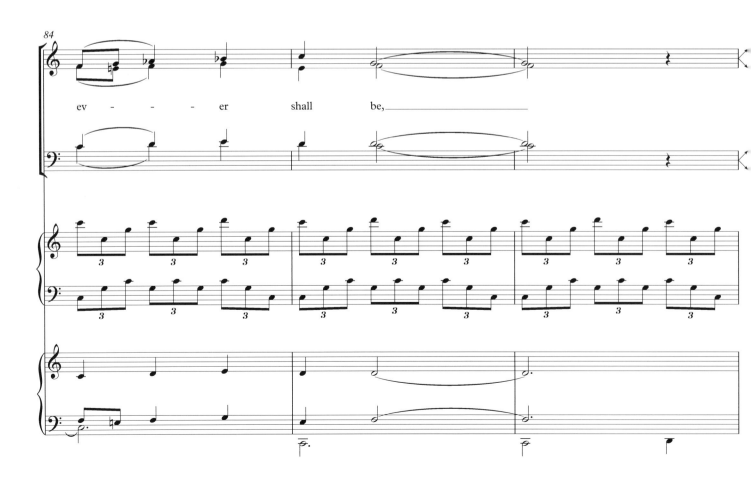

ev - - er shall be, _____

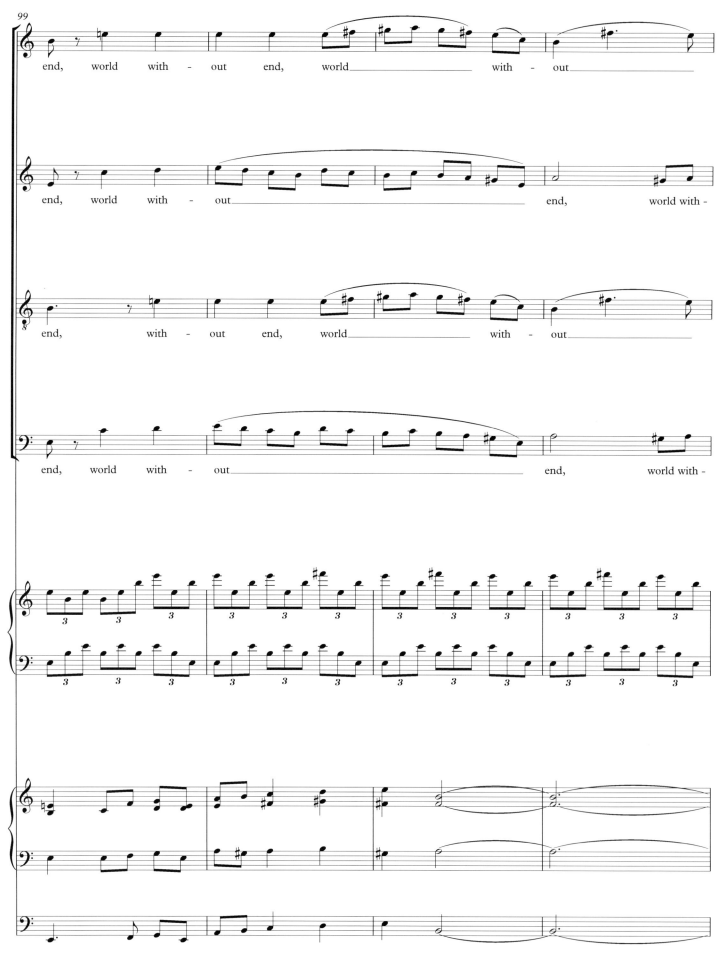

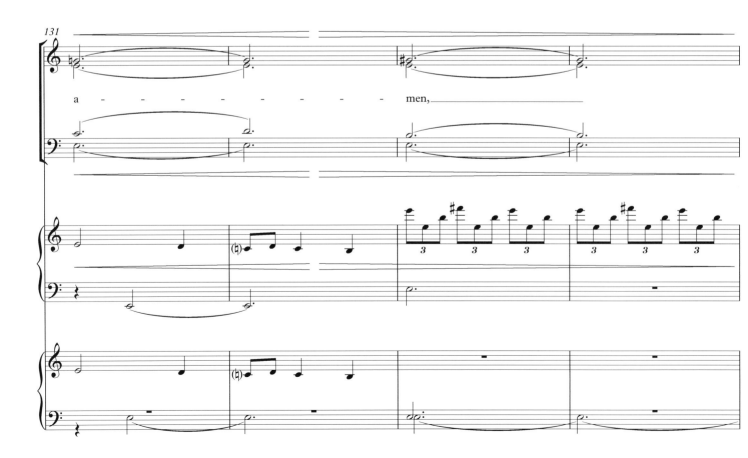

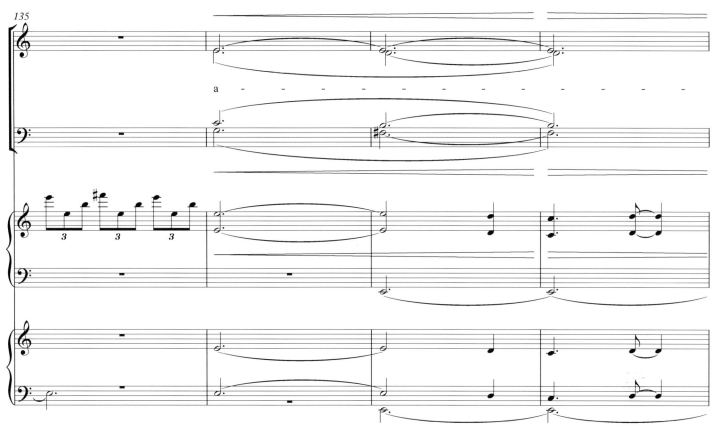

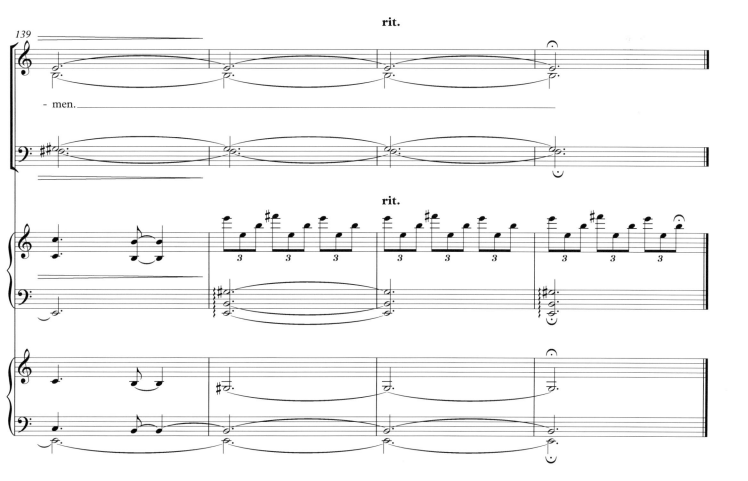